Utopians in Love

poems by

Bob Sykora

Utopians in Love

Cover design by Catherine Weiss

Edited by Ryan DiPetta and Josh Savory

www.gameoverbooks.com

The Sky Doesn't Have Any Answers

In Vermont, the trees can barely stand
the end of winter, all their petrified

leaves lie on the ground, eyeing up
at almost broken branches, who will follow

soon and pound the earth with the heft
of their passing. In the dead grass, I wait

for the entire sky to fall down and meet me—
a blanket of blue, or black with so many

freckles. I wait for the crushing infinite
nothing to hug me to death. I'm sorry

if I sound morose but I can't seem
to put my life back in order. I'm looking

for structure in the fringes
of history books. Stories not so much forgotten

as deemed unimportant. I picture
the utopian Charles Fourier growing gray

as he constructed a perfect society, imagined
people in perfect harmony. How did he dream up

such grand community when he died
alone with so many cats? How long

before they found the body? Was it blistered
or rotten? Did the cats get hungry?

Was he furious to find the polar ice caps
never melted into lemonade, his perfect

new world never came to be? Tossing
furniture, thrashing the apartment

until he fell limp on the floor, cat licks
slowly turning into nibbles. Fourier found

utopia in equations, a perfect set
of measurements he mostly obscured

in his writing. Real people put his ideas
into practice, tried building the communes

of his dreams. But all the Fourierist experiments
would droop into dysfunction. The geometry

of perfection was never quite right.
How do you pick up the pieces after utopia

fails? Where do you go? Josiah Warren
turned to anarchy, tried exchanging goods

for time instead of money. Charles J. Guiteau
assassinated President Garfield

after he was kicked out of Oneida.

Muddy potholes

I don't know how to handle pull my car over

on the road home. The mechanic chuckles,
points me to a place to spend the night

on the cheap. The hotel room sweats,
and on the television they're chasing utopia:

it's on HGTV again, CNN, the evening news—
every channel tries to figure out what's wrong,

how to patch up all the holes in our homes,
in our country, in these damn muddy roads.

The ceiling pants all night, New England drools
humid as I close my eyes and dream myself

right back onto the roof of your apartment, when utopia
was sharing shandies with you while a red July

sky set herself behind grumpy old
Boston. You laid down a sheet and I knew

for the first time I really knew I loved you
as we shouted *Fuck Boston* over and over

at the early moon. Utopia was closest to me
then, when it was nowhere near my mind,

the two of us skipping dinner we talked
so late we almost fell asleep up there, the starless sky

groaning. Let's do it again tomorrow
and the next day and maybe Charles Fourier

felt the same way, drunk on ideas
like I felt drunk on possibility. Maybe utopia

can't last because the sky won't sit still
and we're always tumbling through the big freckled

nothing, so bright in Vermont,
barely there in the city.

I wake up

to an anonymous room, blankets kicked off
a damp bed. So little sleep and so much time

has passed and utopia is nowhere to be found.
But the car is fixed, the road is calling,

and up above there is nothing but clouds,
big and gray and lumpy with questions,

barreling on ahead as far as I can see.

*

*Do we—don't we—have more
(he wishes he knew)*

than what we look back to?

- Lloyd Schwartz

*   remember,
we were in the middle
of not talking*

*about love,
about how I open my mouth
and inside there's a small town*

*full of people who believe,
who actually believe*

- A. Van Jordan

I Have My First Vision in the Middle of the Night

A few more hours. The longest night
since the last longest night. Eyes faint

as feathers, but a stirring, a stirring.

I replace one obsession with another.
In this room made for falling—where I carve

new ways I fucked up into the trees

of that summer. An entire ballet of memories
to mutilate. I try turning my thoughts to history,

not love. Imagine a country without fences.

Where hearts could be replaced by marching
out to the woods, marching on and on

in no particular direction, where—and when—

a country could still be invented. Or uninvented.
My heart won't be held down by history. It doesn't care

for war stories. I want to look in the mirror

and see myself as I was. As what I could be.
As if love hadn't led me here, so awake

with all this time to hold and nowhere to put it.

Why Utopia?

according to Various American Utopians

Man is more than meat.[1]
The American People—we
are a nation of flat chests
and round backs, cramped
gait and pale faces. Our brains
and stomachs are overworked.[2]
Cannibalism, yes, the cannibalism
of the United States, and the city
of Boston in the nineteenth century.
I speak of the permanent internal war,
the state of moral incoherence,
the habit of killing and eating
humbler fellow humans.[3] Yahoo
civilization is doomed. The bubble
is most gorgeous before it bursts.
Of the utter terror of our civilization,
man cannot write.[4]

---

[1] Fredrika Bremer, Swedish writer visiting the North American Phalanx, quoted in
Seymour R. Kesten's *Utopian Episodes*, Syracuse University Press, 1993.

[2] *The Harbinger*, Volume I No. 15, 1845, available in the Boston Athenaeum Archives.

[3] *The Harbinger*, Volume IV No. 2, 1846, available in the Boston Athenaeum Archives.

[4] Thomas Lake Harris, quoted in Herbert W Schneider's *A Prophet and a Pilgrim, Being
the Incredible History of Thomas Lake Harris and Laurence Oliphant*, Columbia
University Press, 1942.

I Have My First Vision in the Shower One Morning

This Is the Beginning of Utopia / Its Material Is Time
- Lisa Robertson, *R's Boat*

Here, in the wet dark, I find myself un-
tucking all the memories I meant

to purge. I find myself mouthing
this frumpy, round word. Utopia

is the revision of this life
I've been working on. It's the way

time wobbles when it comes undone.
A ticking I can't scratch just beneath

my skin. It's not a place, but a language
I used to know scorching my tongue.

I could dream it, I swear, but when
my mouth opens the words flop out,

fall limp towards the drain, shivering,
born again right there in the filth

of my own hope. Utopia is the look
you give me in this revised memory.

Where my words, like doomed dumb fish,
always bite, so I reel them back

and somehow the new ones are always right.
Utopia is a song in the soap, when I watch

these new versions of my life. Like the one
where we're always young, always laughing,

taking showers together. The suds grow toes,
slowly start to dance. Little hiccups

on my skin wallop like a preacher,
blaring with possibility. The bubbles

now endless, devour reality,
slippery, blistering, whispering:

if not now, when?[5]

<hr>

[5] From a bottle of Dr. Bronner's Original All-One Magic Soap.

Eighteen Hundred Forty-Five in Retrospect[6]

I'm in a dream. I'm in the future, the 22nd century,
and they've asked me—me!—to write a history

of the present day. What can I say?

In 1845, we regarded war as right
and proper. And when men fought, they ought

to settle it with a duel. If a man insults
you, it was expected you haul out and fight with pistols.

Industry was real, and everywhere. The humbler
classes affected worst. Some men spent so
much of their earnings on liquor
their families could hardly afford food. Reeling to and fro,

they'd fall into gutters, beat their wives and tender ones.
Some men realized enormous sums, unimaginable sums

of wealth. Most of which was used to accumulate even
more. On the other hand, vast numbers–chiefly
in the cities–sunk into a degree of misery unknown
in earlier, more barbarous times. The rich unprecedentedly

rich, and the poor unprecedentedly poor.
And yet in this age, full of ignorance and error,

animated by one ruling spirit—
the spirit of the self—they thought it

a civilized age, looking back with pity upon simpler times.

---

[6] From *The Harbinger* Volume 2, # 6, dated January 17, 1846. Archived copies
of *The Harbinger* can be found at the Boston Athenaeum.

Various American Utopias, Abridged Version[7]

No moment in history or place on the globe has been more crowded with utopian longing and utopian experimentation than the United States in the middle of the nineteenth century. Countless people on both sides of the Atlantic believed that a new and wondrous society was about to take form in the American wilderness. It was a time when the imminence of paradise seemed reasonable to reasonable people.

—Chris Jennings, *Paradise Now*

The Shakers, Niskayuna, NY	1775 - Present
Harmony Society, Harmony, PA	1804 - 1915
Nashoba, Germantown, TN	1825 - 1828
Brook Farm, West Roxbury, MA	1841 - 1846
Hopedale, Milford, MA	1842 - 1868
Fruitlands, Harvard, MA	1843 - 1844
Oneida Community, Oneida, NY	1848 - 1881
Icaria, Denton County, TX	1848 - 1898

The history of the United States is crowded with longing.
The history of the United States is crowded with longing.
The history of the United States is crowded with longing.
The history of the United States is crowded with longing.
The history of the United States is crowded with longing.
The history of the United States is crowded with longing.

---

[7] Each of the communities listed here are referenced in this collection, but there were somewhere around 100 similar utopian experiments across the country throughout the 19th century.

The history of the United States is   longing.
The history of the United States is   longing.
The history of the United States is   longing.
The history of the United States is   longing.
The history of the United States is   longing.
  history   is   longing.
  history   is   longing.
  history   is   longing.
  history   is   longing.
The history of the United States is   longing.
The history of the United States is crowded with longing.

Longing for paradise crowded the beliefs of reasonable people.

    Reasonable people longing for experimentation.

Experimentation seemed reasonable to reasonable people.

    The United States is no paradise to reasonable people.

        The United States longs to form the globe.

      No utopian moment takes form in the United States.

    No utopian society takes form in reasonable experimentation.

No utopian form seems reasonable to the reasonable people of society.

    Countless people long for paradise in place of society.

    Countless people long for experimentation.

New, wondrous experimentation in the middle of reasonable society.

      Society is crowded.

Crowded with longing.

Reasonable society forms in the American longing.

Society seemed reasonable.

History seemed reasonable.

Time seemed reasonable.

No people seem reasonable in utopia.

No society seems reasonable in utopia.

No American utopia is believable.

I Have My First Vision on the Drunk Walk Home

Someplace different   where time is   tangible and everything   is always

   happening at once, I open up   the little closet

in the back of the house and peek into the library of one Ms. Palmer Peabody,

   where it's Boston, 1840,   and George and Sophia Ripley

are first proposing   utopia   to the Transcendental Club.

   Rewiring conventions, unplugging   history. I nod along

with Emerson, Hawthorne,   other nonbelievers. While in the next room, you

and me are in love, six months   ago, mouths   agape as the country

   undresses on the television.   Bares its rug burns, its scabs,

its infected wounds.   All the levers are being pulled.   A pasty white sludge

runs through our imaginations. Pants   pulled down everywhere and I can't

   believe tomorrow   looks like this.   I keep closing

my eyes, charting maps   for the future, but   nothing sticks.

   Nothing unbreaks.   Tomorrow morning, the sun will crawl

   through the curtain,   the alarm will go off   and its rakish ring will say

nothing   is changed. I spent all day   with pen and paper

and so much history   and I just can't get back to that place   where the wide arms

of possibility felt so big   and burning and buzzing   with birdsong.

I spit up on the wall   after my drunk walk home.   I hang a frame around it,

   instead of cleaning the mess.   Little red stars grimace

in the green muck, and I   just can't look away.

*

*How can the brave, clean lines of a new order
emerge from the excremental treasury of the past?*

- Richard Francis, *Transcendental Utopias*

BROOK FARM, 1841-1846

Flipping through the card catalog in the Boston Public Library's Rare Books Room, I came across my first utopia.

Of course, not actually a perfect society. The card read *Brook Farm, American utopia*, the name taken by a group of people tired of the ills of their historical moment.

It was the same summer all my friends were getting married, the summer I traveled to each wedding alone. Then back to Boston, to the library, to occasionally hop in my car and visit the remains of some old, failed utopias.

Back in 1841, the Boston elites of their time got together, bought some land outside the city, tried peeling away modern problems. They hoped they could return to a simpler, better way of life. They tried looking backward, toward tradition, living communally, sustaining themselves with their own agriculture.

They thought they could solve society's problems by returning to the past. But what past? Who was invited? They ignored all the bodies they were building on and leaving behind. In their propaganda papers, *The Dial* and *The Harbinger*, they were generally supportive of abolition and women's rights movements, but rather than address any issue individually, they assumed their big fix, their new (old) way of living, would eventually correct each of society's ills.

Like me, they believed you had to close your eyes to imagine something new. If you narrow your vision enough, you can talk yourself into thinking anything is utopia.

Visiting Utopia # 1

Brook Farm. West Roxbury, MA. 2016.

Picture me in West Roxbury, all buckled up
in dopey bright, utopian garb. Picture my California knees
chattering the whole New England winter, clutching
my brother for warmth upstairs in the Hive. I wouldn't last

a month. Picture me lying in the fields around sunset
before the work is done. The endless zaw of invisible bugs
murmuring in the tall grass. The choked hiccup of my heartbeat
sputtering over thoughts of Abby Morton[9] in the woozy

grass. The shriek of George Ripley[10] when he sees me
lying there, dead limbs growing into the ground,
longing to be left alone, to sing low hymns at the stars
somewhere even farther away. Somewhere I can sit and think.

Picture me and Hawthorne[11], cranky over manure caught
in our nails, matted in our hair. He just wants to write,
hasn't shut up since he got here. A few months complaining
and he's gone. Picture me, 170 years later, circling

the cemeteries that sulk around old Brook Farm. One
building remains, swaying over a path that leads to grass
and headstones, more grass and more headstones,
and a sunset that won't leave me alone.

---

[9] A teacher at Brook Farm
[10] Founder and leader of Brook Farm

The Nature of New Hampshire and Everything

On the road in July, the radio still
playing the same songs. I mash

the buttons for change when I glance
over at the empty passenger seat,

that old brown blotch of spilt
coffee I never cleaned off. Stray

moments of you keep stirring
next to me on the highway: both of us

antsy to piss last summer, or silently
angry, stomachs snarling hostile

while New Hampshire buzzes by.
The sun slumps into the road, one

spectacular white flicker maybe teeth,
maybe eyes, maybe just the sun's

reflection glaring off a big rig
as it hauls hundreds, literally hundreds

of ducklings in tiny cages, tucked
together, blankly taking the world

in as it all rushes by. New Hampshire
at eighty miles per hour, the new

blurry fuzz of reality, like suddenly
grasping the planet's spin in real time.

And maybe one duckling catches
a brief glimpse of me looking

for you in the passenger seat
as the newly darkening universe

tumbles away, and the nature
of New Hampshire and everything

spins and spins and spins.

From the Journals of Nathaniel Hawthorne at Brook Farm[12]

April 13, 1841. West Roxbury, MA.

I've been busy all day, from breakfast 'til
late afternoon. Old Father Time bears down
his heavy head. The air is brisk and still—
effervescent. Each breath hasn't been owned

by the hundred thousand pairs of city lungs.
My breath never belonged to anyone
but me. I laud my stars, paradise rings
in my throat, the unregenerated man

shivers within me. Oh, if I traveled
a thousand miles, I couldn't disappear
from the world more completely. I dwell
without the city's ruckus, no newspaper

to read. It's like I'm on another planet.
I can hardly remember who is president.

---

[12] From *Passages from the American Note-Books of Nathaniel Hawthorne*. Smith,
Elder and Co., 1868.

Fixer Upper

You said HGTV
is your football. Rage,
rage against perfect blonde
couples picking *fucking*
terrible backsplashes,
the same way my father
screams *Are you kidding me?*
whenever the Trojans score.
You said *of course*
it's terrible, but
on the couch with me
on a Sunday in January,
a gentle snow growing
outside as unstylish
rich couples bicker
through *un-ac-ceptable*
green tile and purple paint
and gigantic decorative clocks,
you can forget everything
for a while. You click
mute and turn sternly
as the next perfect couple
browses short sales in Buffalo.
We could afford that.
Like, right now. The cat
lodges herself between us
as we criticize their choices,
the way they effortlessly
ruin a Victorian. The snow
picks up outside,
the neighbors squeal
over a touchdown,
and a home in Buffalo
we'll never own buries
its head deeper, gray little
hands scurrying through
the snow. Without making
a sound, it disappears.

The Rejected Lover's Sympathy Group[13]

Brook Farm. West Roxbury MA.
March 9, 1845.

The fiddler has arrived—I hear his scraping
all solemncolly afternoon. Painting
lamp shades six, seven hours a day.
Painting a picture frame for Fred—he came
by and read to me for hours. I can't
think of Fred as married—as *belonging*
to any*one*. So much less happiness
in my future than for these ecstatic
lovers. The bewildering birdsong, dizzy
with sweetness. Why do people want to marry?
Maybe, in full harmony there won't be
marriage, or we'll have something very different.
We'll discuss tonight back at the smoky old
hive, whenever the fiddler's song expires.

---

[13] From the letters of Marianne Dwight to Anna QT Parsons found in Marianne
Dwight Orvis' *Letters from Brook Farm*, Vassar College, 1928.

Dogtopia[14]

Under so much fluorescent lighting, all I can hear
is the screech and yowl of pups as they watch
and whimper from their hotel of plexiglass cages. Dog-
topia: endless aisles of toys and snacks and rubber brother
pups to chew on. Good dogs and mean
dogs, ruffled from a recent bath, all watching a kiss

between my brother and his fiancé. I've seen them kiss
plenty of times, but not like this, here
in such celebration of domesticity, all the means
to care for their dog, Linus—*watch*
how his left paw heals. If it bothers
him, he may need these tiny doggy

slippers. Limping on fragile feet, dogged,
deliberate steps towards his people parents kissing,
Linus begins to feel like a brother.
Scared and hurt in the blinding bright, here
in this neighborhood of neons and noises, all washed
out by its own abundance. What does any of it mean?

I roam the aisles, attacked twice by well-meaning
employees. I count all the ways we care for our dogs
I'd never bother with for myself. Linus watches
me disappear down a row of meat treats he longs to gnarl, to kiss.
And I float further away from here,
from all the puppy orbs and sweaters, my brother

and this beautiful life he's built for himself. My brother
calls my name. I can still hear all the mean
things I said to him when we were boys. Can hear
the shrill of my young crackling voice, like a small dog
snapping when he's left outside. I remember kisses
I never had, watching

television. So much television. Watching,
practicing with a pillow, praying my brother
wouldn't walk in. Who would ever kiss
this boy, lost near the leashes, who was so mean
to his brother? What would the dogs
think, if they could hear

what I'd said to my brother when we were boys? Their dog
doesn't understand words, or what it means when they kiss,
but here, under all these lights, he can't stop watching.

Cities

On the other hand, what absurdity can be imagined greater than the institution of cities? They originated not in love, but in war. It was war that drove men together in multitudes, and compelled them to stand so close, and build walls around them.

- Elizabeth Palmer Peabody[15]

What absurdity can be imagined greater than institutions? In what men can great cities be imagined? In what war can love be imagined? What compelled men to build cities around absurdity? What love drives men to war? Men imagined war together in great cities. In great, closed cities, men can imagine absurd institutions around love. Institutions compel men to war in the absurd walls built so close around hand-built cities. Compelled to war, men hand city walls to the multitudes to build greater institutions. Driven together into cities, love built walls around war, so close to what the hands imagined. Cities originated so close to absurdity. Love can be imagined in the walls built around them. Hands in the war drove men to love great absurdities. Men love not in war but in institutions. Absurd war in close cities compelled men to build walls. But hands in other hands built love, and together closed institutions of absurdity.

---

[15] From "Plan of the West Roxbury Community," *The Dial*, January 1842.
    Archived copies of *The Dial* can be found at the Boston Athenaeum.

To Kevin on the Occasion of His Wedding

The Park Street Church's steeple[16] stares
at me through a library window. Its point

pierces the sky so the day droops down
through a tiny tear and leaks all over

my books. Between me and the needle
is a cemetery. So many cemeteries

out here. So many thin tombstones,
winged skulls wink back and forth

until the afternoon dies. It's June and, Kevin,
you're getting married soon. I'm coming

alone, sharing a hotel room with Chris,
wishing Idaho was forever. I'll rewrite

this note after breakfast the day before,
surrounded by the snug choke of our friends,

stories that don't end, and outside a sun
that smells too sweet blushing into mountains.

The sky all kinds of never, and your face
redder than it's ever been. Please, don't

throw this note away. I'm sorry the check
I'm writing is so small. I'm spinning

into a pleasant drunk already, several
months early. Clunky Boston barely exists

---

[16] 1 Park St, Boston, MA

as I walk home. A light pollution red sky
breathes me in. Let's stay here then,

when you're always about to get married
and the summer can pretend it doesn't know how to end.

The Fire[17]

Brook Farm. West Roxbury, MA.
4 AM. March 4, 1846.

The day is still and beautiful, all goes
on so calmly, like a strange dream. How grand,
last night, how leisurely the column of smoke rose
straight to heaven. There was no wind.

It ascended with fiery sparks, glowing
colors rolling as it spangled and tinged,
wreathing solemn and graceful up—up. Flowering,
immense, a clear blue flame mingled

like liquid turquoise and topaz. I could see
from our house—smoldering, magnificent
temple of molten gold. Then the beams
fell, and one after another went

the chimneys. Seven thousand dollars
of cinder. You can't think how it struck
me last night, watching the flames for hours.
Toward the close of the fireworks,

I looked up to the sky and saw Orion—
the unchanging, the eternal—
so quiet, steadily looking down.

---

[17] From the letters of Marianne Dwight to Anna QT Parsons found in Marianne
Dwight Orvis' *Letters from Brook Farm*, Vassar College, 1928.

*E-U-*Topia (Good Place)

The rental car about to burst. The morning after
the wedding. B.O. and beer farts, all parties

too nauseous to notice. Even the mountains
look parched. They judge, they glare over the desert.

A vast rash of dry, dead brown. A topography
of yearning, hungover itself. I thought I saw

utopia last night, holding my best friend
as he cried drunk and petrified with love.

But today utopia is the rest stop where I puke
before buying Cheetos and coconut water.

And it's there, when I fall asleep
on Anna's shoulder. She's too nice to tell me

how much I drooled. The desert stops us twice.
Once, with a hail so hard we could hardly make out

the road ahead. And then, the slow swerve
of another car into our lane—I could see

the glowing columns sway, an endless neon
skyline ready to tumble— but Lindsay's calm

at the wheel keeps us safe, jerks me from a utopia
I can't quite remember.

*

*The entrance to paradise is still
through the straight and narrow gate of self-denial*

- Bronson Alcott, founder of Fruitlands[18]

*Good spirits will not live where there is dirt.
There are no slovens or sluts in heaven.*

- Mother Ann Lee, founder of the Shakers[19]

---

[18] Francis, Richard. *Transcendental Utopias: Individual and Community at Brook Farm, Fruitlands, and Walden.* Cornell University Press, 1997.

[19] Jennings, Chris. *Paradise Now: The Story of American Utopianism.* Random House. 2016.

THE SHAKERS, 1774-Present

FRUITLANDS, 1843-1843

Though they had little in common, the Fruitlands Museum in Harvard, MA is now home to the original farmhouse where Bronson Alcott[20] founded his short-lived commune, as well as the relocated home where a nearby Shaker[21] community once lived.

Like so many things that summer, I drove there alone.

The Shakers are perhaps most known for their namesake—the possessed dancing that at times was a part of their prayer—and their minimalist style of furniture, influenced by their belief that adornment was prideful. They often took in the poor, orphans, single mothers. Anyone who joined was asked to contribute. They tried to be entirely self-sufficient, build a new world by becoming free from the old one. Separation from society was next to celibacy among their chief principles. They thought marriage was selfish, generated corruption and jealousy, encouraged the imperfect animal nature in man.

Similarly, Fruitlands demanded its few members be celibate. Their entire philosophy was rooted in denial. Ridding themselves of the evils of this world wouldn't just return them to a former way of life, but the Garden of Eden itself could be restored. They abstained from eating meat, from using anything produced by or from animals. Even potatoes they dismissed for bending toward the ground instead of upwards to worship the lord.

Both thought, like me on the road alone all summer, that something could be found in denial. That saying the word no to oneself, and to others, had the power to create and build. That we could be better if we just stripped ourselves enough, retreated further and further away.

---

[20] Yes, as in Louisa May Alcott's father.
[21] Officially the United Society of Believers in Christ's Second Appearing.

Visiting Utopia # 2

Fruitlands. Harvard, MA. 2016.

Tucked in the attic at Fruitlands,
dust whirls like static in the sunlight
that cuts through the roof's ancient holes.
I can't stand upright under the low
ceiling where the Alcott sisters slept.
The little life of dust in the light
reminds me softly that it's not so dark
outside, where Massachusetts offers
an endless blue sky, a laughing,
unbearably blue blue all over
the valley, where Bronson Alcott
brought his family to revive Eden,
eating only plants, as if our diet
could save us. Some stray noises call
from the train tracks, all this boundlessness
demands some meaning. All this blue,
all these big thoughts I keep stumbling over
on the path around the property. A small sign
describes a river overflowing through the hillside
in winters past. All those big thoughts
swallowed under water, Alcott's Eden
floating away, like the day does,
curling slow into an attic dark night.

Blueberries

This is the utopia

       where I kissed you

on that pier
on the lake
in the dark.

       What's a pier even for

if not for kissing?

       Would this all be different

if we had kissed?

       Would we wake up

new?

The headlines all celebrate the end
of our calamity. They're serving victory

blueberries on every street corner.
The mouths and hands of every child

are blue. All our attempts to topple
the assholes up top failed,

but they fell over anyway.
And it rained money for days,

but we didn't need money anymore.
There were just so many blueberries.

And when we kissed, we'd share
all our blues. And when we held hands

or hugged or high fived anyone,
we passed it on. And in this great blue

mess, somehow, we all knew each other.
Every hand, every smile was blue.

Everyone must have hugged or kissed or held
someone we knew. The sky in comparison

was so soft and light and barely—
but our hands, our faces, our teeth,

stains in our clothes, the whole street
smothered in a crushed dark blue. The leftovers

piled up on the corner. We're building mountains
from the blue mush. We're shoveling it all

in the backs of pickup trucks, driving way way out
and dumping it into the lake, where you and me

we sat and watched the busy waves and the growing blue
glow of dragonflies hovering under a yellow moon

sinking slowly into the vanishing blue,
where way way down at the bottom

all our leftover blues transform, where they begin
to feed the algae, hungry as hell until renewed

with an electric blue sparkling, and the water
shimmers on and off, so alive,

so powerful, the tides turn suddenly
and crack as they smack against the pier

and it's all because I kissed you

      on the pier on the lake in January
      when it was dark and cold
      and I was scared.

And you could almost see the whole universe

      out there in the dark nothing above the water.

The whole universe was dark and cold and scared,

      and I kissed you anyway.

Anna Alcott at Fruitlands[22]

Fruitlands. Harvard, MA. 1843.

My notebook is heavy with sky. Red
little leaves crumple between my toes.

I place them between brown pages
pacing out the afternoon. No picnic.

No beasts of burden. No beasts
at all. The list of NOs sweats off

the pages. No molasses. No
sugar. No coffee, no tea, no eggs.

No meat. No shoes. No one stays
more than a few weeks. No

more than sixteen of us at a time.
No one young and soft to spy on

when the sun aches orange on the hills.
No butter. My mother doesn't

want to be here. None of us do.
Three sisters cramped in the attic.

No, dad, you can't read my diary.
Where did the pages go? The day

reeks stale in our bunks. The leaves
grow brown and fragile. They shake free

from my notebook and twirl hopeful,
aimless, dead toward the ground.

---

[22] Details from Richard Francis' *Fruitlands: The Alcott Family and their Search for Utopia*,
Yale University Press, 2010.

U-Topia (No Place)

You said my mattress
was too soft. We'd sink
into the middle, swallowed
whole every night, bodies
clunking, angular hard parts
drunk without light. Spelunking
into what? Gruff gnarled breaths
between teeth while the night
spewed her infinite vacancy.
Whenever I'd wake, you'd
already be staring back at me.
Why shouldn't the bed consume us?
Sinking into the dark cavernous
recesses of nowhere, the unimaginable
no place of cold empty space.
What was down there? So soft,
such unbearable, soft nothing.

Visiting Utopia # 3

Shaker House. Harvard, MA. 2016.

A wooden rocking chair sits quiet, untouched
in ages, impossibly small, in the corner. Legs
sawed short for Mother Ann's[23] tiny frame, to rock

her gently to sleep. Each chair built *as if an angel
might sit on it.* A laugh, then a wheeze,
from the older mouth next to me. Then a *please,*

don't touch the medicine cabinet. Here,
the Shakers danced and sang and shook
and didn't have any sex. I almost announce

I've been celibate lately too, but my lips shrivel
like the last time you and me spoke, Boston still-
too-cold-in-April and your feet beating time

in the pavement as you walked away. A beat
whose tremors I still feel today, July boiling,
an hour outside the city, not telling the tour guide

about my sex life. A beat the Shakers may
have danced to in prayer. I ignore this thump
in the walls, my throbbing aloneness, and gaze

at tools two hundred years old for gentle hands
to build delicate seats for angel asses. My ass
isn't worthy. I try moving my feet, but they won't

budge. Sinking into myself, I want to shrink,
hide snug in Mother Ann's rocker, fall asleep
until the Shakers return, and join me moaning

in prayer on the floor. Their yelps reminding me:
maybe my ass is good enough.

---

[23] Mother Ann Lee, founder of the Shakers

Revision

I can feel all the mites
teething at the wires

in my head. Busy little feet
collapsing bridges,

reinforcing the impossibility
of the future. Rubble kicks

around upstairs while we stare
wordless, motionless, at each other

in an already ragged memory.
The first brown birds of spring coo

something I wanted to tell you,
but the blank clouds

had already been pecked
of their meaning. I'm sorry.

I never told you how sorry
I am, how many times

I've relived this moment,
frozen in April, colors

fleeing as the words
disintegrate with the wind's

last gasp. My calendar growls
every time I write the wrong year,

like the mites do, whenever
I try writing some other future.

My hands lose their glow,
my grip snaps the pen,

and a heavy blue smudges out
history, all the lines in my palm.

At New Lebanon They Danced Like Ghosts[24]

Shaker Village. New Lebanon, NY. 1848

I tried to understand it, all this hooting
and tooting like owls in the woods.
You could hear them two miles out. Tuneless
hymns echoed off the endless meadow

for hours. They said they knew I was coming.
They said they'd been waiting. Candles
practiced dying in the window. My feet
practiced falling asleep as they prayed. A quiet

charged with vibrations, oaths and curses
renting the air. Footsteps somewhere and mouths
spewing groans like the night could escape
through their voices. Shooing and hushing out

evil spirits. Swearing at the devils, the boogers,
the sodomites. And all at once, a veil covered
the night, folding into silence heavier than before.
At supper, I ask: *Do you consider yourself perfect?*

One smiles, answers prompt and quiet: *Yes.*

---

[24] Begins with language found in a firsthand account of Shaker prayer described
in *The Harbinger* Volume 5, available in the archives of the Boston
Athenaeum. Continues with language from Clara Endicott Sears'
Gleanings from Old Shaker Journals, Houghton Mifflin, 1916.

The End of History (Chicago Poem)

I was in love
the last time I was here,
where the city slits itself
so eagerly:
the river, the overpass, the train
above belching sparks,
the whole bar below rumbling
with rush hour in its guts.
All these people come and go,
like the years I was young here: my clothes
two sizes too big, my hair so long
with optimism. All these people
holding hands
with the past. The years
passing me by
like little waves
shivering in the glass
as another train storms overhead. Stranger
after stranger outside on the street.
Each looks less
like someone I know, like someone
I'm hoping to see. I swirl
my hopes around, watch them fizzing,
then bring them to my lips
and taste them growing
warm. Is that you
walking by the window in a bulky blue coat?
Or on the train
as it storms past again? Is that all
I can imagine? You,
or someone like you,
passing by in the city I keep coming back to?
There aren't any clear futures

in my beer, on the street,
on the cable news yapping above the bar.
The future is murky
and growing stale. The future
rumbles by again and then the future asks me
if I want anything else
before laying down the check.
And I do—
I do want something else,
but the tv murmurs with the same bad news,
the city outside
stammers with traffic,
and without a thought I will walk
right into it all. Walk
that same walk I've walked
a hundred times before.
I will walk until it's too dark
or too cold or I'm hungry again,
until I find myself
outside the old apartment
trying to make the wrong key fit.

101 Years of Celibacy[25]

Harmony Society[26]. Economy, PA. 1905.

I can count the number
of times we've touched
on two hands plus
two feet, plus your
hands and your feet.
We voted to ban sex
on the same day
as tobacco. Some logic
says an asexual Adam never
tasted his poisonous
fleshy nature until God
ripped the vagina out
from his ribs. Our bodies
just make dust now
at the slightest touch.
Your old lips
hover right off
your face. My old eyes
moan. I can count
the number of times
we've touched
on my hands but
mostly on our feet
under the table at supper—
one kick for yes, two
kicks for no, three
hundred kicks for
I love you will you
meet me out where
the dogwood quake
under the yellow
aspen glow?

---

[25] Based on descriptions in Everett Webber's *Escape to Utopia: The Communal Movement in America*, Hastings House Publishers, 1959.

[26] Founded by George Rapp, this community consisted of a group of Germans who immigrated due to religious persecution for their unconventional beliefs.

Peonies (New York Poem)

I know it was New York and I know
it was summer, but the flowers—
rows and rows of peonies—I'm pretty sure

the flowers were all in my head.
Every storefront filled with peonies, just for you,
and every window had you in its reflection.

The whole city decked out
for some masquerade, and I strolled for hours
uninvited. There it finally was, the Brooklyn Bridge,

and it was no marvel. It was crowded as hell.
It wasn't romantic. A kid ran his bike into me,
I stumbled into an old tourist couple, they tumbled

into someone else's photograph. We were all
unhappy together under the wires.
It was so hot I spent the entire next day

in a museum. It was crowded there too,
everyone wearing peonies in their hair.
Everyone making faces at the past.

Trying to understand each other by staring
at all the ways we wail, the ways we've tried
to turn our messes into something with meaning,

unveiled and boxed or hung on display
to be mostly ignored by sweaty masses.
I got bored. I texted Charles, but we never met up.

I was going to tell him all about you.
Over coffee I dreamt I was going
to tell him about the holes in my pocket,

the parts of the story that I can reach around for
and feel when nothing is actually there.
I had one more night to spend in this city

that kept evading me. Pink petals in every direction,
every street bathed in you, remembering
too much, too well. And for all the big talk about it,

the sun went down the same way
it goes down everywhere: falling so slow
and leaking darkness so faintly I hardly noticed

it take the day away from me. Taking me
further from the days I had with you.
The peonies dried out. Faces withering

in the window. Their petals peered at me
trying to sleep. And the night grew darker,
the dark pungent with memories.

Mother Ann Lee[27]

I really loved and feared her more than any person I ever saw.
                        - Rachel Spencer, Shaker convert[28]

She sweats blood while the night
watches. Little dribbles

of red from her forehead
as she struggles to sleep.

Her cranky body claws
at the stars all jammed

in her skull, tries cleaning the moon
mud stuck on her feet. All the hosts

hide behind her eyes, gently light
little candles, lock up all the cracks

and crevices of the universe.
She greets every day, another miracle,

inventing light wherever she treads. Smiling
vengeance, glowing only as one can

after meeting God, starving
in a prison basement. Knowing

or not knowing she was fed drops
of red wine mixed with milk

---

[27] Based on events described in Chris Jennings' *Paradise Now* (Random House. 2016),
Richard Francis' *Ann the World* (Arcade Pub. 2000) V. F Calverton's *Where
Angels Dared to Tread* (Bobbs-Merrill Company, 1941), and Clara Endicott
Sears' *Gleanings from Old Shaker Journals* (Houghton Mifflin, 1916).

[28] Calverton, V. F. *Where Angels Dared to Tread*. Bobbs-Merrill Company, 1941.

dribbled in a pipe, the small end
tucked through the keyhole

into her dying mouth.
Every day is a miracle,

even if it can be explained.

Utopians in Love

The utopians are in love! They've charted out
the next century, bought these cute matching

uniforms, started peeling the skin off
all our social norms. The utopians are in love!

They grind their bodies against the floor,
pray in new tongues. They sparkle

in their underwear as they wave gravely
at the sunsets in the basement. The utopians

are in love! They're constantly fucking, or never
ever fucking. They decipher the same ancient

phrases for their own purpose, pollute
the country with idealism. They craft

a new life from the words of crazed pastors
who keep getting run out of town.

The utopians are in love and they can't
get enough. They don't tire of barking

across the city, gunking up the country's
gears, dumping ideas for new ideas, always

changing, always thirty colors
at once. Never just fairies or star flowers,

but so many different types of perfection.
The utopians are in love! Busy writing

and rewriting constitutions—they just love
writing constitutions. They're men and women,

sometimes just a few, but always everyone
eventually. The utopians are charged, positive.

The change is coming. The seas will turn
to lemonade, sweep you up, everyone will speak

in blank verse, and everyone, everyone will join.

*

On the whole, I think love is a dangerous thing, and the magnitude of its pernicious influence to be immeasurable. For, as the strict meaning of "love" implies a freedom in the act, I cannot see how it can be proven that all love is not free, and consequently that we are not all free-lovers! Hence I think love an offspring of total depravity. Yes, we have had too much of it already, and the sooner we banish it from our midst, the sooner we shall escape the danger.[29]

—"Professor Snail," Swamp Cottage, September 13, 1858

---

[29] Quote taken from an article titled "Correspondence: Professor Snail on 'Free Love'" found clipped, without original publication information available, at the Boston Athenaeum in archived materials titled "Scrapbook of Clippings Related to the Oneida Community."

ONEIDA COMMUNITY, 1848-1881

The Oneida Community took its name from the town where it was formed, which in turn took its name from the Oneida people whose land this had been. Another thing taken and reused without regard.

The mansion where they lived together is now a museum. A few people still live there, as at least some have continuously since 1862. You can spend a night in one of the rooms where the Oneida utopians lived, so that's what I did.

John Humphrey Noyes founded the community to practice his particular form of "Christian Perfectionism." They were most known in their time for what they called *complex marriage*. Like the Shakers, they believed marriage to be dangerous. They believed no one should be exclusively attached to another person because they were all married to the lord. Using the exact same Biblical passage[30] the Shakers had used to promote celibacy, Noyes offered an opposite interpretation and built a community free from sexual exclusivity.

Of course, he came to this practice after a woman he loved married another man. And of course, their new, supposedly freer set of expectations for sexual relations came with their own set of rules and hierarchies, which, of course, Noyes himself defined.

Like me, even their wildest dreams were still informed by old pain, tethered to old ways of doing things. Even when I do let myself dream, my mind regurgitates the same old desires and fears. Recreates the same reality with slightly different hues.

---

[30] Matthew 22:30: "At the resurrection people will neither marry nor be given in marriage; they will be like the angels in heaven."

Visiting Utopia # 4

Oneida Community Mansion House. Oneida, NY. 2016.

Today, the utopians are buried
next to their various lovers
in the middle of what is now

a golf course. This morning,
I was the only one who showed up
for the 10 AM tour, guided alone

to their tiny bedrooms,
where they wouldn't sleep
together after sleeping together.

From a green couch in the lounge
they could keep track of who
came and went. They criticized

each other, publicly, in a great hall
where today a pamphlet informs me
you can get married, something

they never did. And down the stairs
a tiny yellow room adorned
with rows of metal teeth,

hunting traps sold to fund
their experiment. Rusted but still sharp.
A bear trap, the biggest of them all.

Its gruesome grin like a gateway
beckoning, just as big and somehow
also bigger than you'd imagine.

In the next room, rows of silverware,
which they made instead of traps
after fur hats went out of fashion.

The museum curator tells me
many people visit this old utopia
to see the silverware. Outside,

Junebugs and hours of driving ahead.
Old men in golf shorts ignore me
as I take pictures of tombstones.

Crying on the Exercise Bike
While Watching *The Great British Bakeoff*

It's two in the afternoon and I love you.
It's true, it's two in the afternoon
and the entire room is blurry
with sunlight, with fresh tears.
The cake turned out poorly.
Someone is going home. The layers
crumbled. I love you, and all
your layers. Crumbling, overcooked.
I pedal faster and get nowhere.
Crumbling. Overcooked. Crying,
I don't know why I'm crying—
You're crying because you lost,
because you're going home.
Because next week your baking
won't be judged. Because the cake
was perfect when you practiced.
Because. I pedal faster. I am no
closer to you. My body is soft,
full of cake. I ride my exercise bike
because I hate my body. I watch
reality tv because I hate working out.
There's no cake in the evening.
I love you, even when there's no
cake after the long day. Crumbling.
Overcooked. My body is blurry
at two in the afternoon as I pedal
faster. I pedal nowhere. *I don't know why*
I'm crying. Overcooked. Pedal.
Blurry day. My body was perfect
when I practiced. I pedal faster.

My cake is blurry. The sun
fills the room. The room crumbled.
There is no cake in the evening
after the long day. My body
pedals faster. The day is further
away. It's two in the afternoon.
I don't know why I'm crying.
You are not coming home.

Growing Up at Oneida

according to Pierrepont "Pip" Noyes[31]

I was born and brought up in a strange world. Somewhere,
in the misty dawn of my life, I remember applesauce

over oatmeal in tin porringers. Maroon and pink,
Shockley, the pony on springs, colored with the gloom

of community criticism. Greens and reds outside, the crooked
stump where we climbed and played we were sailors on a ship.

We named one stump Gog, the other Magog. Wormwood tea,
so much molasses. Out at Seymore's strawberry patch

I remember asking for *liberty*, always getting
in some trouble with *liberty*. Our eager mouths

made mistakes for us. Upstairs at the mansion,
a small row of engravings—all the muses: Homer, Socrates,

Pythagoras, Plato. Me and Dick would go hunting
for muskrats. Me and Dick would get punished for *special love*,

spending too much time together. But we never
wanted for nothing. Never thought about possessions.

Never knew children on the outside weren't raised
by a department. We didn't know our parents

were all each other's parents' lovers, coupled up
for breeding, or that family could mean anything

other than all of us, here, together. You know,
a calf has no idea it will ever be a cow.

---

[31] From Pierrepont Noyes' *My Father's House; An Oneida Boyhood*, Farrar & Rinehart,
    1937.

Walden Pond

Concord, MA. 2016.

Walden is mostly bugs and sweat in August.
Flies find crevices I'd long forgotten. They like
the way I sweat, the way my body drains

itself in the sun as the trail opens up to a new
row of condos, another set of railroad tracks.
The tracks call at two children hiking with their father,

a precious summer day they'll faintly
remember when they're older. I go for a swim
instead of barging into their memories.

On my back, staring up at the tippy tops
of trees slicing away the horizon, sealing off
how close this is to reality. I'm peeing

in Walden Pond, my toes don't quite touch
the bottom. But I can almost reach back
to last summer, wearing red shoes, so unsure

about each other. Soft brushes of arms
until one of us dares to grab a hand.
We didn't take a picture because you hate

pictures. That moment doesn't last
because of course it doesn't. Treading water
a year later, and finally a train comes roaring by.

Its call reminds me I'm here, now, and I'm sure
those kids can't hold back their delight
as it storms by and forever away.

From the Journal of Tirzah Noyes at Oneida[32]

Oneida Community Mansion House. Oneida, NY. 1873.

Not quite silent upstairs. Hunched
around the corner from the lounge,

where everyone knows who comes
and goes from anyone's bedroom.

Stern philosophers' faces
hung around the room to judge us.

J.H. Noyes tells me he loves me
again. Words chosen carefully, so pinched

with pressure they might explode
if he sees me distracted, staring

out the window, counting the men
who've told me the same. Counting

the times he told me who I could
or couldn't talk to, or sleep with,

or written letters in my name.
Lovers look as down deep wells. Or

Lovers look as down as deep wells.
Or *[text illegible]*, Edward,

the only one *[several words
unreadable]*. I draw a veil

over last night, I screamed for hours
after community decided for me

[text ends here].

---

[32] Italicized text from *Desire and Duty at Oneida: Tirzah Miller's Intimate Memoir*,
Indiana University Press, 2000.

Sex Laws in the Library

Silence. The dull gaze of books. I'm reading old
sex laws in the library[33]. One hundred forty years ago

John Humphrey Noyes[34] declared *The affections
can be controlled* and today my whole body

balks at the phrase. The books just shrug.
We reject the idea that love is an inevitable

fatality. The reflection in the window turns my face
to rust. The summer outside taunts me, slumped

over the table as the silence squawks, broken
by someone's sneaker. *The whole matter of love*

should be managed. Like I could manage your hundred
different smiles, your teeth grinding at my memory,

chewing through nights we stayed in, dinners
overcooked, laundry sprawled on the apartment floor

while we—*become exclusively attached, to idolize
each other, this is not desirable.* The dwindling sun

wrinkles into the lamp on your nightstand. Exhausted
fingers pull pages over and your bedroom flickers

in the bookshelves. Now the book scowls *Exclusive
attachment is unhealthy and pernicious wherever*

it may exist. I'm sweating a hundred eyes, a hundred
laughs, a hundred small summer nights in your bedroom,

and the book squints, sighs, says: *love
does not mean freedom.*

---

[33] The Boston Athenaeum, 10 and 1/2 Beacon St, Boston, MA 02108
[34] Italicized language from *Hand-book of the Oneida Community*, published in 1875 by
the Office of Oneida Circular, found at the Boston Athenaeum.

No Locks[35]

Nashoba Community[36]. Germantown, Tennessee. 1827.

Fanny Wright says no locks, says locks
mean giving up. Last night, Rederick tromped
into Isabel's room, looking for something
that doesn't belong to him. Locks don't talk,

but they do say something. Locks say
we're unsafe. Locks mean hushing behind doors
at the sound of footsteps. Heavy whispers
in the hallway. The buzz of secrets, separation,

some hefty green unfurling in the walls. Rederick
asks about free love, and Fanny's silent eyes
shake the room. *No locks* doesn't mean
you can just have whatever you want. Everyone

drifts to bed, to their unlocked rooms.
Everyone dreams the same dream: an endless
field of metal, locks blooming raucous smiles,
tangling arms, latching and unlatching, laughing

as the green sky dampens and a dark
impenetrable sea fills the infinity,
and there are no more locks, no more doors,
just a swelling fear that no one is alone anymore.

---

[35] Based on events described in Everett Webber's *Escape to Utopia: The Communal Movement in America*, Hastings House Publishers, 1959.

[36] Founded by Frances "Fanny" Wright, this small community was formed as an experiment in Wright's plan for emancipation, with hopes of both racial and gender equality. While Wright was sick and away from the community, the community's leaders also turned to "free love" as one of their tenets.

Broken Utopia Abecedarian

At first it was just an obsession. All these hours in the library. I didn't think much of it.

But later I found I couldn't help myself. The rabbit hole ran so deep. And without
it, I'd wake to the same tired apartment, the same tired life. The same

cat with her paws in my face, begging me to start my

days.   Once, not even that long ago, men
would look out and see an endless
country, fertile in

every direction. There were so many butterflies, roads taking you wherever you
liked. Or no roads at all. Their words wept sticky with possibility, dribbled
all over everything. You couldn't move your

feet without stepping in the honeyed mess of someone's
imagination.   Once, I was so in love I swear I
could see fields stretch their arms to the sky, let their reach
cover up all the stench of the century, all this blood and

gore on tv, the residue of a sticky-fingered history, men who took and took, drank their
own mythologies to justify all the taking, and today the trauma dressed up and
replayed all across the planet, every night—and I could ignore it all,

hold my breathe to infinity, I was so

in love.

Just for a minute—and it seemed so long, time was unraveling—everything was possible, all

kinds of madness seized me. All the best kinds, the ones where

life swings by like one big

musical. Every day was a song, and every song rejected the word

no.

No, because nothing   is inevitable.

No world   is inevitable.

No life   is inevitable.

No me   is inevitable

Of course, it didn't last. The only inevitable is change. All this pink in my hands, naive to all this quaking,

crumbling history that strokes its beard and says

really, you got your hopes up?

Silly rabbit, utopia is for kids. Love is hardly utopia,

though I can't blame you for the confusion. Of course,

utopia fails. Of course, it can't last.

Utopia—it mocks me, rests its hand on my throat. So many old

utopias gone stale, rotten, their only testimony drying up in dusty pages hidden
in the back of the darkest corner of the stacks.

Utopia,
utopia.

You.
And that feeling.
And all the ways

I've tried to dream it back.

The Doll Revolution[37]

Oneida Community Mansion House. Oneida, NY. 1851.

Their hair burned fastest. Curls scorched
crisp one second then gone as air. Hardly
even smoke as their dresses and vacant

little eyes ignited and popped over wooden
torsos crackling, then disintegrating. We sought
perfection in all things. So why not children?

Why even bother if they aren't perfect
little communists? We formed them, like God
does, from before birth. Chose parents,

ideal combinations—anything is possible
in community. They know nothing outside
the mansion, *complex marriage*, our slice

of perfection. Surrounded by prairies, trees,
an endlessness impossible in the clamor of cities.
The kind of love impossible tied up in that old con

of monogamy. Nonsense foreign to their bright,
brilliant faces. Those perfect red cheeks
that don't belong to any one of us. The love

of a mother we call *special love*. Frowned
upon. Unacceptable. And the kids—so perfect—
they figured that out. With no prodding,

the boys called for a vote: *Dolls teach
motherhood, special love. We should burn
all the dolls.* Almost everyone agreed.

So, they gathered the wooden figures, piled them
out front, and the whole community watched
as flames crept over tiny faces, ragged little

bodies caving into ash. Not crying, as special love
slowly waned in the fire and the wind hushed
so loud you could feel it in your skin.

*

I needed history in order to explain myself.

- Lisa Robertson

Self Portrait as Utopian

When I'm truly beautiful
I'll believe anything. The great

trundle of history eventually
gallops in the right direction,

doesn't it? In a raving field
of books, a great landscape

of wishes, sun bleached
pages flailing and my whole

body elated. The room of myself
all waxy red wires, the stringy

remains of my organs left
burning through the night. I keep

believing, even as the tides
turn back on me. Salt water

spikes my nostrils, spackles
my throat. The whole field

is drenched now. And the sun
looks so tired, limp yellow

bulb, dangling there, chord
exposed, so close to the water.

I still clutch the sacred
scribbles long after the pages

wash out, little holes marring
the words. I look for the sun

through a tear in the page,
I pretend there's an eclipse.

I pretend, like any old thing,
it's a sign.

The Voyage to Icaria[38]

Denton County, TX. 1848.
At Icaria, even the horses only shit
when they're supposed to. C'est
au Texas! was the refrain
when French fiction readers[39] came

to America looking for the paradise
they'd read about. But the desert, all snake
bites and malaria and dysentery—and then
the doctor went mad. One man

was even struck by lightning—could you
believe it gets worse? All this before
finding they were scammed out
of their land. Crossed rivers

on rafts bound with their belts.
Boiled pigeon for dinner. Mud
huts. Sunburn groping their bodies
as they waited patiently

for their companions to join them
in this suffering. Waiting for Icaria
to materialize before their bodies
gave in to dust, dissolving in the hell

they'd found instead. They'd move
to Illinois before finally settling.
Every morning, a shot of whiskey
before hitting the fields. Eyes dark

and whimpering at the work ahead.
The awful orange heaving all over
everything. Maybe paradise exists
only if you had to struggle for it.

---

[38] Based on descriptions in Chris Jennings' *Paradise Now* (Random House. 2016.)
and William Alfred Hinds' *American Communities* (Office of
the American Socialist, 1878).

[39] Yes, this utopian community was inspired by a novel, Étienne Cabet's *Voyage to Icaria*
(1840).

E-U-Chronia (Good Time)

When will it be then? When
will the old skin finally flake
free, expose the ripe peach
of each shoulder's blade, fresh

pink flesh ready for wings
to emerge from the wounds
like blind worms gulping for life
through mud after heavy rain?

When will the stars wear out?
The heavens unhemmed, the earth
groans so loud we all walk outside
to find the shape of the sky

is finally telling us exactly
what to do. Will I know it's time?
What will it look like when the new
age stares me in the face? My lips

tired, eyes stale. Me, a remnant
of the now that's best forgotten.
Will you wait for me, if I totter
behind, like I always do?

Hesitating at the rope bridge
as it sways and sways. The gap
below barking, the great dawn
ahead still hasn't risen, and I

am afraid, I am so afraid, I won't
even notice when it comes.

Various Other Utopias

This is the utopia where there are no people there are only cats
all calamity of fur and cuteness we're climbing towers made of carpet
we're licking each other clean we're taking naps in the sunroom all afternoon
drinking milk knocking over houseplants
we're sashaying away not looking over our shoulders
there's no need for the old oops did I do that because
everyone else is also a cat and they're all too busy huffing away at snacks
or asleep again I swear we're always sleeping we're all too busy
with dreams to get swept away in some nonsense like love
like history like utopia like yada yada yada
have you ever even slept right up against the window
the sun hot on your ass like the whole damn universe
was intent on you feeling safe and comfortable and warm
I tell you one time I was thinking about the future
right there on the windowpane
but then the sun got all just right on my ass
like sleeping inside a toaster oven like being little spoon
to the whole galaxy like I can't even explain it
but that for me was enough

but this is the utopia where online job applications
do not require you to fill in tiny boxes
with the exact same information you included
on the pdf resumé you already submitted
of course this is hardly a utopia because the tyranny
of labor under capitalism exists just the same as it does
in our own contemporary condition
still everything in this utopia is just a tiny bit better
because we've been freed from those tedious moments grinding our teeth
feverishly retyping the same information about our boring lives
into blinking tiny boxes on the screens we rely on
for both labor and leisure
everyone has saved
a number of hours of their lives
some have even found entire new days
of freedom not having to retype their resumés
into tiny boxes and therefore
their utopias like everything else
are a little bit better than the ones you and I can dream
they imagine so much cooperation four day work weeks
no jobs at all
and the people in the utopias of their dreams can dream
even bigger more impossible utopias
and the people in those utopias can dream
utopias so far removed from what you or I
could imagine it would break our brains
if they were described to us right now
but these people
not retyping their resumés into tiny boxes
are mostly content not to dream
because their world is good enough or as good as it will ever be
considering what history
presented them with
even here they sometimes feel simply helpless
to make any real change

       but this is the utopia where no one wonders
if they are loved no one wonders because there's a great big bell tower
in the middle of town and every hour on the hour
the bells ring out:

I LOVE YOU

and at noon
or at midnight
whenever
things are worst the loneliest among us
can be found gathered up on the hill that stares over the whole town
the tower
in the center the echo just right
and twelve times we're all reminded:

I LOVE YOU I LOVE YOU I LOVE YOU I LOVE YOU
I LOVE YOU I LOVE YOU I LOVE YOU I LOVE YOU
I LOVE YOU I LOVE YOU I LOVE YOU I LOVE YOU

and this town is like any other
we've got all the same problems and fears
but up there on the hill even on the coldest nights
I promise you'll find them at least someone
huddled in a blue coat watching their breath's smoke
waiting for the tower to call to remind them

but this is the utopia

where there's no history no one paging through old diaries
or sweating hunched over in a library
like me at the archives of the Boston Athenaeum
just barely catching a sweat droplet from my forehead
headed for a page 200 years old everything here is so stuffy
except for that one guy who casually brings his dog
up to the silent floor every morning in this utopia the historian
is out of a job there's nothing in the pages the vaults have all been emptied
they let you walk inside and hear the echo of how much we've forgotten
the echo like a voice inside you when you're driving alone toward the ocean
with no real direction the echo like a voice at night when you're twelve
and camping with the scouts and you're unsure
if you're more afraid of the voice or of waking your father
what's a library even for if we have no history no one bothered
to write this mess down and on the other side looking in
I can't tell if they're better off in this utopia
if the blank pages of the spineless books
give them a freedom I've never known
the empty pages whisper opportunity the empty pages
say go go go go go the empty pages say hallelujah
with the archives full of nothing the historian
writes histories of the future there's no story to retell
I'm not sure if it's some sort of cultural amnesia
or some law against history books the utopias all look so muddled
through the looking glass I thought they'd all be crystal clear like snow globes
I thought the utopias would open up something inside me
I thought the utopians had something to tell me
but all afternoon in the Athenaeum
I was paging through books and documents
I was trying to go deeper and deeper into the past
I was trying to be overtaken by an obsession
and around every corner tucked in the stacks in the middle of every book
there was a memory of you smiling
there was a love I couldn't hang up
there was a lump in my gut
there was an amethyst in there deep down
I swear somewhere sparkling inside me
if I could just capture something in all these old stories if I could just find

80

the great secret if the utopians could show me the way
I could mine that old amethyst lump
growing stale in my guts I could smash the rock
right there on the big long table in the middle of the silent floor of the library
the August sun lighting up that rock that purple sparkling
the crash startles all the patrons with their headphones in
and the dog starts barking under the table
oh it would be out of me it would be out my body
and it would be glowing
I would exorcize the thing
and for once I would be marvelous
I could get the hell out of there and forget all this history
I could wipe the smudge out from the snow globe
I could smash that snow globe open on the amethyst
and see the little people inside
how they have no history but they're all still there
rushing around together picking up the pieces
and trying to build something beautiful

but this is the utopia
where I never thought to equate utopia
with love where I didn't spend years trying to force
a metaphor this is the utopia where I don't equate utopia
with anyone this is the utopia where the poems really do open up
new worlds the utopia where my country's history books are filled
with more utopians where I don't have to gloss over so much awful
to find a few people who ignored all that same awful whenever they tried
to dream this is the utopia where I can write my fears into submission
where I don't get so scared I have to reboot my life in a new city every few years
the hours aren't so hollow and ringing with echoes of thoughts I thought
I'd beaten down moved past all those echoes of me second and third guessing myself
this is the utopia where I never spent so much time in the past
where my utopias are all future and sometimes even right here in this moment
that I'm spending with you
this utopia doesn't require so much
turning back and squinting
in this utopia all my utopias are vibrant
all alive with so many bugs so many gardens you wouldn't believe
how many blueberries I tell you
after all this searching all this writing and remembering
all I really want from a utopia
is one where the utopias I dream
aren't so mundane

Visiting Utopia # 5

Sabbath Day Lake Shaker Village, New Gloucester, ME. 2017.

There are two Shakers
left.

    Maine cuts a bitter
cold. Wrong turns slink
me around a bend
where a lake of ice glows
impossibly, like utopia
was right there beneath us
the whole time. Its gleam
briefly blinding for both me
and the off-course ducks
overhead.

    There were three,
but Sister Frances passed
just after the new year.

Up the road, tucked
in the snow's blaring
white, a single tombstone
stands thick, terse. It reads
simply: SHAKERS. As if
ready for the dream
to end.

    Instead, scattered
gray goats chomp at the sky,
idly milling on the hill
over a sea of trees.
They ignore the sun's
roar, all this pristine
country sparkling,
asleep, under a grave
of thick white sheets.

The trees whisper something
to the sky, something about
permanence.

             Up
in the brick house,
a small community gathers
quietly for service. Most
of their prayers are song,
and their songs buck
at that tombstone, buck
at history, swaddling the dream
with their voices.

             Listen:
their song lingers out
the window, past the frozen,
perfect lake, past the animals'
blissful disinterest, past
the tombstone's heavy glare.
The songs don't demolish
the tombstone but turn it
on its head. Standing stark
now, like a flag, it announces
we're still here, still afloat
by some grace, some specter
of possibility. Its small whisper
twisting into my ear, itching
under my skin as I drive on again
in silence.

Notes

Page 6: "The Sky Has No Answers" was written after a trip to Vermont and a short stay with my friends Kevin and Annie in their yurt and owes its existence to both that trip and the conversation between Rachel Zucker and Ross Gay on episode 25 of the Commonplace Podcast.

Page 10: From Lloyd Schwartz's "No Orpheus" in *Cairo Traffic* (2000) and A. Van Jordan's "Remembrance" in *Quantum Lyric* (2004).

Page 16: The latter half of this poem owes its form to Robin Coste Lewis' poem "verga:".

Page 30: This poem also owes its form to Robin Coste Lewis' "verga:".

Pages 37 & 43: "Visiting Utopia # 2" and "Visiting Utopia # 3" were written after a visit to the Fruitlands Museum in Harvard, MA, where both the Fruitlands house and a Shaker residence are open to visitors.

Page 58: "Visiting Utopia # 4" was written after a one-night stay and tour at the Oneida Community Mansion House.

Page 72: From the poem "Face" in Lisa Robertson's *R's Boat* (2010).

Page 83: "Visiting Utopia #5" was written after attending services at the Sabbath Lake Shaker Village, home to the last practicing Shakers, a community that was incredibly generous and warm.

Head to utopiansinlove.com for more.

Acknowledgements

Many, many thanks to the editors of journals in which poems from this collection first appeared, sometimes in slightly different versions: *Cotton Xenomorph*, *Dead Peasants*, *Footnote: A Literary Journal of History*, *Glass: A Journal of Poetry*, *Ghost City Press*, *Gulf Stream Lit*, *IDK Magazine*, *Longleaf Review*, *Maudlin House*, *Peach Mag*, *Pine Hills Review*, *Public Pool*, *Reality Hands*, *Reservoir Lit*, *The Shallow Ends*, *The Shore*, *Third Point Press*, *Vagabond City Lit*, and *Woven Tale Press*.

This book wouldn't have been possible without a generous fellowship from the Boston Athenaeum, where much of the research for this book was initially done in the summer of 2016.

So much gratitude to everyone at UMass Boston for inspiring the earliest inklings of this project and reading its very earliest drafts, especially Jill McDonough, Joyce Peseroff, and Lloyd Schwartz, who were the first people that made any of this feel possible, to my cohort: Kate Glavin, Emily Jaeger, Aly Pierce, and August Smith, who have fingerprints all over these poems, and to all the other folks in the program whose friendship and conversation made that time in my life so special, particularly Dave, Danya, Emily, Justin, and Elysia.

And to the many folks who graciously read early versions of this manuscript along the way: Diannely Antigua, Eloisa Amezcua, Zack Bond, Michelle Betters, Chris Corlew, Allison Dikanovic, Emily Jaeger, Marcus Meej Khoury, John Leo, Christopher Morgan, stephanie roberts, Adrian Sobol, and Kevin Weidner. Your eyes and thoughtfulness with the work was so vital to me sticking with it.

Thank you to Diannely, Jill, Alina, and Maya for your blurbs, and more importantly the kindness and enthusiasm that came along with reading and seeing the work as you did.

Thank you to Josh and everyone at Game Over Books for giving this collection a chance, and to Catherine Weiss for seeing this book so well in designing the cover art.

And so much continued gratitude to the many, many people who have inspired and loved and supported me in all the ways that need to happen for me to even think about writing poems: To both Jeff and Julia and Kevin and Kate for letting me into your homes when this book was just getting started and I was so lost. To my Chicago friends who have loved me no matter how many times I've left, especially Smags, Kevin, and Anuj for being the first people who made me want to take my notebook out and actually share my bad poems, and Chris for wanting to talk to me about poems to an imagined audience every month. To Thomas, Ryan, Ashley, and Christina for still being the most solid, warm people in my life. To everyone who has made Kansas City feel like home, especially Abby Bland and Melissa Ferrer Civil for being my newest first readers and making me feel like I could do it here. To Allison, for getting it so well and so immediately and making an expansive view feel so easy. To Oma and Opa always. To Mom and Dad and the rest of my family–where to even start? Thank you thank you thank you.

Biography

Bob Sykora is the author of the chapbook *I Was Talking About Love—You Are Talking About Geography* (Nostrovia! 2016) and the collection *Utopians in Love* (Game Over Books 2025). A graduate of the UMass Boston MFA program, he now lives and teaches in Kansas City. He can be found online at bobsykora.com.